WHY HE CHOSE HER OVER YOU

How to get over it and move on with your life

PAUL ELIZABETH

Table of contents

INTRODUCTION

If you're wondering why he chose her over you, it's one of the dumbest feelings in the world...you're not alone. Many women were there. Not only does it feel like a punch in the stomach, but being with reality for a while makes it worse than a normal rejection or breakup. It makes you doubt yourself. You compare yourself to other girls. It also shows the rift between you and another girl who is not very feminist, making you feel guilty. It can take over your mind, wondering why he chose her over you. So it's clear that you want an answer as to why he chose her over you.

Why does it hurt so much when you drop it? Before we get into why he chose her over you, let's explore why it hurts so much. You might have cared for him and loved him. I want my loved ones to protect me too. Just because he did doesn't mean your feelings go away. And when he chooses someone over you, it feels like you're not good enough. Not only do you feel like you've failed him, you feel like you've failed yourself. Women have fought each other for years in society, so being left for another woman sucks. We are conditioned to get mad and upset at other girls, not guys.

Swallow your feelings for him - anger, sadness, pain - and focus on the other woman. We can't be mad at him, so we still care for him. Think bachelor's degree. The girls are constantly fighting each other instead of questioning the main character's actions and decisions. It makes more sense to ask him what he really wants instead of comparing himself to the opposite girl he's clearly in a relationship with. However, it is our nature to blame ourselves for failed relationships. And the way social media works has allowed us to literally compare ourselves to the woman of his choice. Or you can see what she looks like in a bathing suit or how awkward she was as a teenager. You can mock her girlfriend or be intimidated by her girlfriend. All of this adds to your anxiety and makes you feel worse. Can you imagine? All that pain and self-doubt because he chose her over you?

Why he chose her girlfriend over you? Answering this question is as easy as asking it, but most people aren't considerate enough to give us an answer. Not that his answer was really meaningful. If you could ask your ex why he chose her over you, what do you think he would say? Would he say she's hotter? Is she easier to use, or more fun? Or will he say you failed? Will he say the worst thing you think about yourself? Honestly, most men don't even see themselves wondering. I can assure you that he didn't choose her over you because your nose is dented or your breasts aren't the same size. Or not because you weren't curvy enough. It wasn't because you weren't confident enough, comfortable enough, or laid back. As much as we are comparing, wondering, worrying, and stressing about all this, he chose her over you for some unexplainable reason.

When someone leaves you for another woman, it's pure taste and emotion, at least for half-hearted men. It won't happen. Recall the Bachelor show for a moment. He had two wives and when he had trouble deciding, he didn't say one was tall and the other was short. He talks about your future, the lifestyle that matches him, and how he has this indescribable feeling. And that's the problem. It probably won't give you rest. It's not about sticking to, focusing on, or breaking apart your body or personality, but it's the way it is. Just because he feels that way about someone else instead of you doesn't make you less awesome. It doesn't mean you are not qualified. It means you weren't there for him, and that's okay. Think like pink hair. Cool. You may not like it personally or think about it at all, but that doesn't mean there is anything wrong with the other person. Just because he didn't choose you, doesn't mean you aren't great or a suitable partner for someone else.

How To Get Over Why He Chose Her Over You. This answer probably didn't help much. Yes, it's a pity that there is no clear and concise answer to something like this. Seriously, there were a lot of people there. The good news is they're over it. So are you. It's not an overnight healing process. It's hard to understand that the guy you're in love with chose someone over you. There are some things you can do to get over it and move forward.

CHAPTER ONE

Look back

You need to do a lot of self-reflection and distance yourself from the feelings you still have for him. Ask yourself why you think he's great. Be careful of his and your actions in the relationship. Then look at the situation with new eyes and a new perspective. Relationships may not be as good as you think.

Not personally

As I said above, it's not about you. She's not "better" than you. So this is not something most people don't experience on a daily basis. You are not the only one who has been "rejected".

Remember his bad

This may sound a little strange, but I miss my ex because I remember all the good things about him. But guess what? There must have been some downsides, too. The first bad thing is he left you, right? So instead of focusing on what you like about him, focus on what you don't like about him.

Focus on your strengths

On the other hand, focus on what you love. You're probably cute, kind, funny, selfless, and the list goes on. Don't keep looking for things that make him dislike you. If he is blind and does not see your beauty, he loses! Whether you're already thin or need to lose a few pounds, getting fit after a breakup is always helpful. Start eating better or losing weight if necessary. .Hit the gym and put your health first. After a while, look in the mirror and see how much he's lost.

CHAPTER TWO

Hang out with friends

Good friends are with us in good times and bad. After all, that's what they're for, right? So keep busy and go out with your friends. Eat lunch, go to the cinema, dance, and get distracted with friends as much as possible.

Pamper yourself

You deserve to be taken care of. Going through a breakup is not easy, so please give me the time I need. Get a massage, try a new hairstyle, do whatever makes you feel calm and happy.

Don't overdo it

You might want to sit on the couch with a gallon of ice cream, a bottle of wine, and your favorite Netflix show from her. However, if you indulge yourself in something too much, you may be reluctant to try again. Excessive indulgence in alcohol, food, or anything else will not help you get over it. It will only mask the pain temporarily.

CHAPTER THREE

Do not contact

Sure, you want to talk to him. You want an answer as to why he chose her over you. But keeping in touch with him just makes me feel worse, even though I thought it would make me feel better. So please don't contact me no matter how hard it is.

Clean up your memories

When you're in a relationship, you tend to post pictures around the house and on the phone, even wearing your favorite T- shirt to bed. Having her around just reminds him that he's not there either.

Don't stalk him on social media

Everyone stalks people on her social media. But you really have to resist the temptation to stalk him and her girlfriend in cyberspace, maybe your curiosity is trying to get the best of you, but do you really want to know? So don't torture yourself by following all their steps.

Don't Post Revenge

Similarly, do not post passive-aggressive or overtly aggressive revenge posts on social media. It doesn't make him feel guilty, it just makes you look bad. Keep your negative emotions.

Talk to family and therapists

If it's really hard to move on, it's wise to talk to someone. It's great, so if you can afford it, see a therapist. If you can't do that, talk to an older and wiser family member and help them put the breakup in perspective.

Start dating again

As the saying goes, "If you fall off your horse, get back on your feet!" In other words, back in the dating world. Once you get the attention of another man, it's much easier to get over him. It will help you take your mind off things and finally find the right man for you... someone who appreciates you and won't let you go

CHAPTER FOUR

Conclusion

Eventually, you'll realize that you don't want someone who doesn't want you, for whatever reason. You might waste a lot of time wondering if she's a better kisser than you, or if she's more interesting than you. But it wasn't about her. And it's not even about you. If he doesn't want you because he chose her, or for any other reason, you're definitely better off without him. Dealing with pain, betrayal, and self-doubt practically and rationally isn't easy, but over time you'll realize that it's better if someone chose you first. I hope you can stop wondering why he chose her over you. Instead, ask yourself what you would choose over him now.

www.ingramcontent.com/pod-product-compliance
Lightning Source LLC
LaVergne TN
LVHW020546160826
845677LV00015B/4223

9798352347003

Book by
Prof. Lucy Russell

TABLE OF CONTENTS

INTRODUCTION

As a man, there's a brutal truth that I need to concede: most men are horrendous at being a tease.

Are there special cases for that standard? Obviously.

When a man is battling to play with a young lady, there generally is a smooth Brazilian helicopter pilot close by who can dip in and discuss anything.

In any case, that doesn't mean everything trust is lost, fellows. To know how to get a young lady to like you, being a tease isn't the response. That sounds counter-useful, yet there's just that far can get with a lady by perseveringly seeking after her. On the off chance that she wasn't keen on the primary spot, she will stop that super quick.

The key is causing her to do an equivalent portion of the work. You want to make a young lady need you however much you need her.

Yet, how would you truly achieve that? How you truly do persuade a lady that she ought to be drawn to you? Assuming you're battling to sort out some way to draw in ladies, toward the finish of this book you will comprehend how to get your preferred lady.

THING LADIES NEED IN A RELATIONSHIP

It will help you identify various needs of a woman, which will enable you to able to know about the need of a woman. It's not generally simple to parse out what the individual sitting opposite you needs seeing someone. Certainly, you could constantly ask the lady you're dating what she needs (and as a matter of fact, you ought to), yet can we just be real for a moment: That is more difficult than one might expect. To give those inquisitive a glance at what ladies need from men, here's a decent spot to begin. Simply recollect: Each individual is unique, so this rundown ought to be the establishment on which you can construct. Address the issues of the lady in your life (or the lady you might want to have in your life), it will require investment, exertion, and trust.

- **Communication and honesty**

Additionally, assuming you would like your assistant to make sense of their necessities clearly to you, they might be feeling the same thing about your correspondence style. Correspondence is one of the significant needs and needs seeing someone. This goes for both all through the room. Furthermore, you will find that frequently an incredible discussion will prompt an extraordinary second between the sheets. Not at all like men, what ladies need in a relationship is to feel sincerely bound to their accomplice to appreciate sex. A profound conversation where there is an incredible this way and that of feelings can be breathtaking foreplay. Furthermore, once in bed, don't be modest about proceeding with the conversation — yet have it zeroed in on your common actual joys as opposed to, say, legislative issues. Remember that how you speak with your life partner in marriage reflects how agreeable your relationship would be.

- **Tune into her emotions and her words**

At the point when both of you are somewhere down in conversation, it is essential to pay attention to what she is talking about as well as to hear the feelings underneath her words.

Could it be said that she is restless, exhausted, miserable, irritated, or baffled? Or on the other hand, on the more sure side, would she say she is cheerful, upbeat, giggly, and senseless?

Ladies' correspondence styles incorporate far beyond being verbal, so be mindful of the profound messages she is conveying to understand everything about what she is imparting.

- **Signs Of Certainty**

Conviction means clearness, at last. Assuming that you're sure about a person or thing, you'll be clear about it in your viewpoints, words, and activities. It will decipher your way of behaving. What is lucidity? I want to suggest this conversation starter because a ton of times individuals are muddled… see what I did there? Being clear is tied in with knowing the significance of an individual in your life and trying to show it to them, in any capacity you know. In some cases, it requires working it out; at different times, it's more about following through with something. At the point when you're clear in your mind about an individual, you will naturally show it.

Therefore, fundamental thought processes are. Presently, don't misinterpret this because numerous ladies have no cognizant thought of what drives them or what their intentions are; it's simply how nature has wired them.

Be that as it may, similarly as the need might arise to understand what drives her, you want to quit agonizing over it appearing to be legit. It is never going to sound good to us since we unexpectedly see things. However, on the off chance that you understand what her buttons are, you will want to play sweet music that she will not have the option to stand up to.

Remember knowledge is power and you like power, isn't that right? Indeed, realize what drives ladies and afterward, you will possess a great deal of it.

ATTRACTION

One thing we want to take a gander at is the idea of fascination. Fascination will decide if you get a date. The uplifting news, however, is that ladies are more drawn to the character than they look. While looks do assume a part, on the off chance that you have the perfect character qualities, ladies will in any case be drawn to you regardless of whether you're not a Brad Pitt copy.

In this way, assuming your reason as of not long ago has been that you're not rich, well known, or Brad, then, at that point, you should understand that it's just a reason. While ladies

might be drawn to the rich and well-known, the character wins out and on the off chance that you have the certainty and humor that ladies love, you will win like clockwork, regardless of the size of your ledger.

The far superior news is that these are everything that can be picked up, implying that you can make yourself more alluring to ladies by developing the sort of character they would be drawn to.

If you are faltering and muttering that you shouldn't need to change for a lady to be drawn to you and that she ought to like you for what your identity is, then awaken and take a whiff of reality since everybody needs to change. We are changing all through our lives and we have two options: we either let life shape us or we channel the change to help us.

In any case, simply recall that fascination is not a decision. Dislike a lady will see a fellow and size him up, then, at that point, tick off his characteristics and out of nowhere choose "I decide to be drawn to him since he is steady,

dependent and has steady employment." It just doesn't work that way since, supposing that it did then you most likely would not need to read this book.

Fascination is very natural, and that intends that if she isn't drawn to you after the first date, then there is little you can do about it since you will be nothing over a companion to her. Regardless of the number of presents you get her or the number of eateries you take her to, she isn't going to foster a fascination for you abruptly. You're in an ideal situation just continuing.

WHAT FASCINATES A WOMAN TOWARD A MAN

The issue with most men is that when they are around alluring ladies they want to acquire their endorsement by being excessively great, considerate, etc. The issue is that this sets her in the situation to lead and assuming she is driving she won't ever feel that flash of fascination for you. As referenced beforehand, ladies are drawn to areas of strength for certain men and a solid person won't ever permit a lady to lead.

Entertainingly enough, the most ideal way to start that fire of fascination isn't to require her endorsement and to show her so much. Try to make her work for your consideration as opposed to the reverse way around. This will unbalance her cool and reserved way to deal with men basically because you are accomplishing something so unforeseen and strange she will be frustrated not to essentially be interested in you.

The more you seem as if you needn't bother with her endorsement, the more certain you will show up and certainty is extremely alluring to all kinds of people. Thus, the more you can act in each circumstance, the more alluring you will be.

Nonetheless, remember that there is a barely recognizable difference between certainty and pomposity.

While presumption might be interesting partially, a lot of it will make you seem to be an all-out jerk.

THE REASON

Most folks who fizzle with ladies generally have a reason, however more often than not that excuse is just in their minds. The fundamental explanation a great deal of folks fizzle is a direct result of how they think which affects their way of behaving.

For instance, if you imagine that you won't ever get an opportunity at conversing with an alluring lady then your activities will be by your viewpoints. You will radiate "frightened" energy and you likely even won't move toward a lady.

Then again, the more sure you are in your capacities to engage and draw in a lady, the more grounded you will show up and the more alluring you will be. More often than not the deficiencies we envision have prevented us from acting and they are so profoundly imbued in our minds that we don't for even a moment acknowledge we have them.

the most effective way for you to conquer this issue is, first, with just enough soul looking. You need to distinguish what the reason is that has been keeping you down so you can manage it. Then, you want to teach yourself about ladies so you understand what ignites that sensation of fascination.

When you come to see precisely the exact thing ladies want then you will want to extend an atmosphere of solidarity that they will see as totally powerful. Each lady has a young lady within her yearning to be secured and focused on and that young lady is the person who will have the last word. On the off chance that you start to figure out that young lady and address her, showing her that you are in charge of every part of your life, then, at that point, ladies will be drawn to you like a moth drawn to.

Yet, you need to acknowledge the way that you can improve and it is an option for you to turn out to be more appealing to ladies. Disregard the reasons that nature hasn't blessed you with Apollo's excellence or that you can't contend because you're not running a Fortune 500 organization. You want to stop the self-indulgence and begin seeing for the last time that on the off chance that you can encourage a lady then you will prevail upon any stud with a Ferrari assuming he has the character of a wet cloth.

Personality Traits Women Find Irresistible

There are sure character qualities that you can develop which ladies see as totally powerful. Indeed ladies will be drawn in and remain drawn to a man who can encourage her when she is with him or is considering him. This implies that your character is your most remarkable resource since you can utilize it to encourage them.

For instance, one thing ladies love is a man with a comical inclination. The more you can make her snicker, the more she will need to invest energy with you. Moreover, ladies are drawn to insightful men, particularly the people who know how to utilize that knowledge to astonish them and connect with them.

Training is another strong weapon you can utilize because ladies love to hear tales about individuals or spots. Not exclusively will you generally have a point to discuss yet it will be something intriguing that draws in her somewhat similar exhausting repetition themes most folks discuss, similar to her #1 variety or where she works.

Ladies are likewise drawn to predominant men, regardless of whether they understand it. Naturally, ladies have been designed to look for the insurance of a male, and the more predominant the man, the better the opportunity he has at safeguarding her. In any case, don't botch being prevailing with being controlling. You want to overwhelm the circumstances in your day-to-day existence as opposed to being controlling of her and removing her singularity.

Insightful men are additionally extremely alluring to ladies. Ladies aren't thrilled when they get a gift due to the actual gift but since it is verification that you were considering them. The gift is just an image so any showcase of the way that you were pondering her will encourage her, regardless of whether it is to tell her you were troubled that she went out with one more person for lunch.

If you have any desire to truly dazzle a lady, then, at that point, you want to figure out how to see subtleties. Ladies invest a ton of energy doing right by certain they, so if she has a pleasant haircut, it was anything but a mishap. She isn't wearing that hot dress because the closet fell on her by the same token. She is attempting to intrigue you and assuming you notice these subtleties she will be incredibly dazzled that you saw her endeavors to be appealing to you.

Ladies additionally like men who are forceful, yet not as in you won't take no for a response. That is called date assault.

No, forceful men that ladies like are the people who understand what they need throughout everyday life and they pursue it with all that they have and won't stop until they accomplish their objective.

As we have proactively referenced, ladies love a sure man and, surprisingly, somewhat presumptuous. Once more, don't mistake this for being pompous. The right demeanor is a ton of certainty joined with humor. in

different words you are sure to the point that you might chuckle at yourself without feeling unreliable.

UNCERTAINTY IS THE GREATEST MOOD KILLER

Quite possibly the greatest deterrent, men face is instability. This is the one thing that will deliver you ugly to any lady. Ladies can recognize uncertainty and poverty right away and there's nothing that will switch her off very as much as a shaky person.

A man who feels awkward in a specific circumstance or is awkward with what his identity is will seem to be uncertain. He might attempt to seem sure, yet very clear is just a demonstration since he is attempting to acquire endorsement simultaneously through what he says or how he acts.

A few instances of the uncertain way of behaving incorporate permitting others to pursue the choices. Thus, assuming you are continuously hanging tight for her to conclude what you will do or where you will be going she will think you are unreliable. Ladies like it when men conclude what will occur and afterward, they just make it happen. To accomplish something different, she will tell you yet don't necessarily anticipate that she should pursue the choices.

One more way you appear to be unreliable is by assuming you are continually squabbling over everything. Regardless of whether you are correct, it simply causes you to seem unreliable and you need to contend with each easily overlooked detail just to demonstrate you are correct.

You likewise need to abstain from swarming a lady at the outset or being too emotional. You should be somewhat more easygoing and allow her to become all right with you or she will think you are unreliable. Assuming you are continually contacting her she will either think you just need to get her into bed or that you are apprehensive she will take off.

WOMEN AND SEX

How about we get something straight? Ladies love sex similarly as much as men. Society has just made it a no point except for the reality of the situation is that ladies appreciate sex and, indeed, they discuss it with their sweethearts constantly. All right, the facts confirm that they aren't however focused as men seem to be nevertheless they actually will wind up attractively attracted to a talented man's sweetheart.

Finding a man who knows how to satisfy a lady in bed is difficult, as most folks are very childish in this division. Ladies are not the same as men with regards to sexual delight and their psyche should be involved similarly however much their body or there won't be any firecrackers.

Most folks simply race through it, without understanding that it takes significantly more than a "wham, bang, thank you ma'am" to satisfy a lady in bed.

You want to mark the word foreplay into your mind with a red, hot poker since, supposing that you get the foreplay right, ladies will not have the option to help themselves. You will wind up beating them off with a stick.

Foreplay is more than sex, every one of the little subtleties will get her creative mind started up and needing more. It's about very much positioned contacts when you are out with her, it's about delicately telling her what you would like to do with her even though you are open, it's tied in with setting the temperament and building the expectation. The more sexual strain and the expectation you fabricate, the faster she will soften in your arms.

How does this influence your capacity to date any young lady? Ladies get on things like this rapidly because they are experts at perusing non-verbal communication. Furthermore, a man who knows how to satisfy a lady oozes a specific certainty that says "I will shake your reality" and ladies can get on that.

By turning into an expert at satisfying ladies, you won't simply turn out to be more alluring to ladies, yet you will likewise keep up with that fascination.

All things considered, a gifted sweetheart is an interesting product and they won't have any desire to let you go.

APPEARANCE

Indeed, ladies are more drawn to the character as opposed to looks, however, this doesn't imply that you shouldn't make yourself as satisfactory as could be expected d. This is because ladies go with a ton of choices in light of tiny subtleties. For instance, on the off chance that you are excessively nonchalantly dressed, she will think you are just too sluggish to even consider caring for yourself and accordingly will likely have an unkempt home and you would presumably introduce a lot of work for her to be a mess with. On the opposite finish of the range, assuming you exaggerate your appearance and look excessively set up, she will consequently feel that you most likely invest more energy before the mirror than she does and she would rather not date somebody who is keener on himself than on her. Indeed, getting the right equilibrium is somewhat interesting yet as long as you care for yourself and that incorporates losing the paunch, you will find that more ladies will be drawn to you. You should simply get a magazine and see what's in design, put in a couple of dollars on some new garments, and away you go. However, one thing is without a doubt. On the off chance that you circumvent wearing some better pants and you look nine months pregnant, you can be sure that appealing ladies won't allow you a subsequent look. It boils down to the way that ladies require some investment to make themselves more alluring to men, and it requires a great deal of investment and work, so they expect a similar thought in kind, which is regular. In this way, if you truly need to have the option to date any young lady then you want to start thinking responsibly, fail to remember the six pack consistently, and hit the exercise center. What's more, don't begin whimpering that you can never seem to be the muscle-bound studs that are on the front of romance books. Nobody anticipates that you should, however, you can get yourself in shape which won't just assist you with making more progress with ladies yet you'll likewise be better which means you'll have more years to appreciate life

WHY SHOULD I CHANGE?

All things considered, you don't need to change if you would rather not. Nobody is compelling you to make it happen. Be that as it may, you should contemplate whether it merits the work if you have any desire to have the option to date any young lady, regardless of how appealing she is. Truly we don't live ideally and regardless of whether you

maintain that she should like you for what your identity is, regardless of how you look then you will have a major issue.

Alluring ladies are moved by such countless men that they need to utilize the external appearance of a man to rapidly conclude whether he merits her time. They judge the kind of individual you depend on the picture you present and they will be unable to look past an overweight and ungroomed appearance as well as an all-out absence of culture. It's likewise a question of confidence. Do you have so little regard for yourself that you believe you're not worth getting to the next level? Buy a couple of books, get on the web and find out somewhat about what's happening on the planet, have a shower consistently, get your hair managed, go to the exercise center, and out of nowhere you will find that your certainty will skyrocket too.

The thing is, that is not evident. At times changing yourself is great for a relationship — as a matter of fact, frequently it's totally important. Connections depend on a compromise because, regardless of romantic comedy dreams, there is no such thing as a "wonderful fit" between individuals. There are some "nearly there" fits and "beautiful darn close" fits, however, you're never going to find somebody who just so ends up adjusting precisely to the existence you've laid out as a solitary individual. There will be off-kilter points and sharp edges between you and your accomplice that must be pared down, formed and shaped so you can fit all together in a consistent unit. A large number of these progressions will happen normally throughout your relationship; others will be more diligently changes, changes that require a ton of work from both of you.

This is a precarious subject to expound on because there is a scarcely discernible difference between great change — a change that makes you and your accomplice more joyful and more grounded as a couple — and self-destruction. There are things you shouldn't change about yourself, and there are explanations behind what you shouldn't change. You ought to never allow yourself to accept things like, "If by some stroke of good luck I were unique, this individual would adore me." That logic is damaging and insufficient; your accomplice ought to cherish you for your center self since that center — your spirit, your embodiment, anything you desire to call it — won't change. Yet, what can change — and what frequently needs to change — is how you connect with your accomplice and your opinion of yourself on the planet.

FEAR OF FAILURE

What is fear of failure? The fear of failure is the tendency to do nothing due to the worry of failing. The same fear stands like a tall wall between you and your goals preventing you from taking any action. The most concerning issue men have is that they neglect to make a move given an apprehension about disappointment. We are essentially incapacitated by the feeling of dread toward dismissal such a lot that we would prefer not to make any move whatsoever. Peculiarly, numerous men will stroll into a high gamble circumstance without the slightest hesitation, like a battle, while we are deadened by the prospect of conversing with an appealing lady. For instance "*Your lady colleague who recently joined is the most beautiful girl you have ever met. You experience all the unicorns and the rainbows when she walks by. Yet, you cannot gather the guts to walk up to her and strike a conversation. Think about this: she isn't your girlfriend now and she will never be if you do not talk to her. But the fear of trying and failing stops you before you even take the first step. Do you think what would follow if she turned you down? Your friends would make fun of you, she would never make eye contact with you and her friends would giggle at you.*

You prefer staying single because the fear of humiliation is harder to bear than the joy of having a gorgeous girlfriend."

In a battle you are most certainly going to encounter some actual aggravation yet we are more terrified of moving toward an alluring lady than we are of getting into a battle, even though the most terrible that can happen is that she will say no. However, imagine a scenario where you succeed.

WHERE TO MEET A WOMAN

Tracking down spots to meet ladies isn't quite as hard as you could suspect, particularly if you begin thinking a little fresh. Fundamentally, you want to go to similar spots they go, and that doesn't mean simply going down to the bar for 16 ounces.

In the first place, you need to settle on what sort of lady you might want to date. For instance, you could need a lady who is into working out, so then, at that point, you ought to join an exercise center. If you are searching for a party young lady, go out to clubs. Nonetheless, do recollect that there are loads of folks competing for their focus in settings like bars.

The thought is to just plunk down and contemplate where your ideal sort of lady would probably hang out and afterward begin going there. Ladies likewise want "unintentionally" to meet a man in a typical, unforeseen spot. The supermarket, book shop, or shopping center are a few genuine models.

The rundown of choices of where you can meet ladies is practically boundless. You simply need to utilize your knowledge and imagination a little bit.

HOW TO MEET A WOMAN

Ladies can smell a conversation starter pretty far and they don't answer well enough. The issue is that while you may be a certifiable person who has been strictly concentrating on his dating guide on the most proficient method to get ladies, she will just think that you are either a player or powerless.

Smooth conversation starters generally turn on the alerts for most ladies since they assume they are being played. Also, the way that she has most likely as of now been let by fifty different folks know how lovely her eyes are won't help what is happening much by the same token. Thus, the key is to stand apart from the group.

The main thing you shouldn't do is assume they have no clue about the thing you are doing. Let me tell you that it's a game you will fizzle at. Ladies are like hunters about smelling your shortcomings and your goals. They can smell what you need well in advance since they are seasoned veterans at perusing non-verbal communication. You will offer yourself before you utter the main syllable and afterward, you are ill-fated to fall flat.

Then again, as opposed to attempting to conceal that you are endeavoring to get her, get perfect at it and you will not need to stow away any longer.

Keep in mind, presumptuous certainty and humor are a strong blend that you can use for your potential benefit.

OUT WITH CONVERSATION STARTERS, IN WITH DISCUSSION

One of the most concerning issues with conversation starters is that they are an obvious indicator of the way that you are apprehensive. The conveyance is substantially more significant than what you say. On the off chance that you are cool, sure, and gathered you could recount the phone directory and she would, in any case, think that you are alluring. Then again on the off chance that you stammer over a pre-practiced conversation starter, you are plainly showing that you are apprehensive, which won't win you any focus.

Once more, as opposed to getting going with some messy conversation starter, your possibilities increment ten times on the off chance that you draw in her in a fascinating point, asking her perspective. This functions admirably if you request that she express her viewpoint on a disputable subject you are bantering with a companion. One, she will be bound to answer since ladies could do without being inconsiderate for it, and two, it's an extraordinary method for bringing her into a lengthier discussion which will permit her to see who you truly are.

If you just find out if you can get her a beverage or not, she can say "No, much obliged," and leave. Nonetheless, on the off chance that you find out if ladies acquire less in the work environment than men doing likewise work since you have been discussing it with your companion, you will ignite her advantage and she is bound to stay close by and contend her point.

THE TELEPHONE NUMBER AND EMAIL ADDRESS

Oddly enough, most ladies are more open to giving out email addresses, than their phone numbers. What's more, as a matter of fact,

email is a greatly improved method for getting going the discussion since they likewise will more often than not become a little far off on the telephone.

By utilizing email she will be more OK with you as she will acquire a little about the edge of your thought process. She will likewise be satisfied that you required some investment to contemplate what you will share with her. One more incredible thing about email is that she will be bound to answer an email since you are bound to contact her than by calling her. Furthermore, she can reply whenever, not at the event that you call her and she is working or in a gathering.

The key to requesting a telephone number or an email address is to utilize a little humor and certainty. For instance, an extraordinary method for receiving an email address is to find out if she an has email or not. At the point when she answers indeed, takes out a piece of paper and pen and passes them to her, basically accepting her yes as an acknowledgment to give it to him.

Then, while she is thinking you can attempt to inspire her to record her number also, or, hold on to get her musings emails. Since ladies see little gamble in giving out their Emails because that badgering by email is very improbable, you are normally in an ideal situation trading a couple of messages first and afterward requesting her number.

Indeed, you need to seem sure while requesting her email, along these lines, to develop your certainty, essentially work on getting telephone numbers and messages from ladies. You can go to the shopping center consistently and practice so you can move past your apprehension about dismissal. The more dismissals you get, the less they will influence you.

CONCLUSION

To have the date option for any young lady, regardless of how appealing she is, then, at that point, you want to develop the character qualities that she views as alluring even though a few people are brought into the world with these characteristics, they can be learned, and since ladies are more drawn to a man's character and how he affects her than his looks, there is no deterrent in your way other than yourself.

If you figure out how to dispose of your restricting convictions, your certainty will develop, which will make you substantially more appealing to ladies. A lady will go out with a normal-looking person that has a fair monetary arrangement instantly over a rich incredible-looking person if the previous causes her to feel superb while the last option behaves like a jerk.

Keep in mind, the main thing remaining among you and accomplishment with ladies is you. Figure out how to be more alluring to ladies and you will find that nothing can hinder you.

TIPS THAT WILL GUIDE YOU IN DATING ANY GIRL OF YOUR CHOICE

- Look approachable.
- Dress well.
- Be complimentary.
- Make eye contact.

- Make sure that when she talks to you, you continue the conversation.
- Be yourself.
- Quit trying hard.
- Allow her to notice you.
- Prepare your mind to approach her.
- Don't be predictable
- Try to impress her.
- Be dominance.
- Have a good sense of humor.
- Give her space sometimes.

www.ingramcontent.com/pod-product-compliance
Lightning Source LLC
LaVergne TN
LVHW020536160826
845677LV00015B/4093
9798355214258